Meditations

Chiara Lubich

Meditations

New City

London   Dublin

First Published as *Meditazioni* 1959
by Città Nuova, Rome.

First published in Great Britain 1971
Revised edition 1985
Second revision 1989
Published in Great Britain 1989
by New City
57 Twyford Avenue, London W3 9PZ

British Cataloguing in Publication Data

Lubich, Chiara 1920–
 Meditations, – 2nd rev. ed.
 1. Christian life
 I. Title. II (Meditazioni) English
 248.4

ISBN 0-904287-29-7

Cover picture 'Touch of Life'
by Anton Krajnc

Typeset in Great Britain by Chippendale Type
Otley, West Yorkshire

Printed and bound in Great Britain by Biddles Ltd
Guildford, Surrey

Contents

Introduction

Chiara Lubich's *Meditations* are fast becoming considered by many people to be spiritual classics. They have something in them for everyone.

Yet many readers when they first come to Chiara Lubich's *Meditations* find themselves with a mixture of feelings. They are intrigued, delighted and occasionally baffled. A strange quality of darkness and light characterizes the writings. In a sense they dazzle us.

The reason is not that the *Meditations* are complicated. In fact they are extremely simple, and the ideas they contain are beautifully and lucidly expressed. But they have a depth of meaning at times so different from the normal way we reason about things, that they seem strange, almost from another world. And in a way they are. They express, very clearly, something of heaven's viewpoint. And the human and heavenly way of seeing things rarely coincide.

Perhaps it is useful, therefore, to have an idea of how to read these writings. Certainly, they need to be looked at with care, but it is also helpful to be aware that they express thoughts that, while making the heart leap for joy and the spirit sigh with relief at finding words that give life, sometimes leave the mind puzzled. But not for long. The ideas, if profound, are simple; all that is needed is to practise as much as has been understood, and sooner or later the depths of meaning start to become clear.

The most common experience when reading these *Meditations* is that they open up a dialogue with the Eternal, and the reader finds a new logic, the heavenly way of reasoning, begins to filter into the soul. We feel that we become better, and we discover a yearning, almost a homesickness, for heaven. And that turns us to face our everyday life, with its everyday struggles and all our everyday neighbours, with renewed resolution. We wish to care for others in the most realistic and down-to-earth way possible.

Indeed, we feel enabled to take part in fulfilling the driving theme in the *Meditations*, the prayer with which Jesus summed up his life-work, uttered to his Father the night before he died: 'May they all be one.' (John 17:21.) In short, these *Meditations* lead us on an adventure into God.

A Note on the Translation

The present edition of *Meditations* is a new translation. It incorporates and builds on previous translations from the original Italian into English, but it sets out to improve upon them in a number of ways.

Where there were mistaken renderings of the original, these have been corrected. Where the original text has been revised, so has the translation; thus the present version attempts to be the closest yet in English to the author's own wishes.

This translation, furthermore, does something new. It tries to capture the style and flavour of the original, even down to mirroring some of the rhythms and surprising turns of phrase that give such zest and freshness to the original. Where Chiara Lubich is poetic, so the translation is poetic; where she is telegraphic and laconic, so is the translation; where her sentences flow on, so do the translation's. All this, of course, within the limitations of writing sensible and comprehensible English.

This new version, therefore, is possibly as near as can be reached to how Chiara Lubich might express herself if she were to write in

English. It is a sensitive and literary work, yet full of the simplicity of the original *Meditations*, and as such, it is well suited to helping them lead the reader on an adventure into God.

Heaven and earth will pass away

And I realize more and more that 'heaven and earth will pass away . . .' (Mark 13:31), but God's plan for us does not pass. The only thing that fully satisfies us is to see that we are at every moment where God, from all eternity, meant us to be.

The attraction of modern times

This is the great attraction
of modern times:
to penetrate to the highest contemplation
whilst mingling with everyone,
as one person next to others.

I would say even more:
to lose oneself in the crowd
in order to fill it with the divine,
like a piece of bread
dipped in wine.

I would say even more:
made sharers in God's plans
for humanity,
to embroider patterns of light on the crowd,
and at the same time to share
shame, hunger, troubles
and brief joys with our neighbour.

Because the attraction
of our times, as of all times,
is Jesus and Mary,
the highest conceivable expression
of the human and the divine:
the Word of God, a carpenter's son;
the Seat of Wisdom, a mother at home.

The cross

'Let him take up his cross . . . ' (Matt. 16:24).
These words are strange and unique. Like all the words said by Jesus, they have something in them of a light that this world does not know. They are so bright that the dull eyes of human beings, including those of apathetic Christians, are dazzled and therefore made blind.

There is nothing, perhaps, more enigmatic, more difficult to grasp than the cross; it does not penetrate the head and the heart of human beings. It does not penetrate because it is not understood, because often we have become Christians only in name, merely baptized, maybe practising, yet immensely far from being what Jesus would like us to be.

We hear about the cross in Lent, we kiss it on Good Friday and sometimes hang it up in our rooms. It is the sign that seals many of our activities. Yet it is not understood.

And perhaps the whole mistake lies here: in the world, *love* is not understood.

Love is the finest of words, but it is also the most deformed and debased. It is the essence of God, the life of the children of God, the breath of the Christian, and it has become the heritage, the monopoly of the world. It is on the lips of those who have no right to use it.

Certainly, in the world, not all love is like this. There still exist, for instance, the feelings of mothers which, because they are mingled with suffering, make love noble. There is fraternal love, marital love, filial love, which are good and wholesome. They are traces, although perhaps unconscious, of the Love of the Father, Creator of all things.

But what is not understood is love *par excellence*: which is to understand that God, who made us, came on earth as one human being among others, lived with us, and allowed himself to be nailed to a cross: to save us.

It is too high, too beautiful, too divine, too little human, too bloodstained, painful, intense to be understood.

Perhaps maternal love can give us an inkling of it. For the love of a mother is not only caresses and kisses; it is above all sacrifice.

Thus it is with Jesus: love impelled him to the cross, considered foolishness by many.

But only this foolishness has saved humanity and has formed the saints.

Saints, in fact, are people who are able to understand the cross. They are men and women who, following Jesus, the God-man, have taken up their daily cross as the most precious thing on earth. At times they have brandished it like a weapon, as soldiers of God. They have loved it all their lives, and they have known and experienced that the cross is *the key*, the only key to a treasure, *the* treasure. The cross gradually opens souls to union with God. Then, through human beings, God once more reappears on the scene of this earth. He repeats – although in a way that is infinitely lesser, though *similar* – the actions that he himself once performed when, as one human being among others, he blessed those who cursed him, forgave those who insulted him, saved, cured, preached the words of heaven, fed the hungry, founded a new society based on the law of love, and revealed the power of the One who sent him.

In short, the cross is the necessary instrument by which the divine penetrates the human, and a human being participates more fully in the life of God, and is raised up from the kingdom of this world to the kingdom of heaven.

But we must 'take up our cross . . . ', wake up in the morning expecting it, and knowing that only by means of it can we receive those gifts which the world does not have: that peace, that joy, that knowledge of the things of heaven, unknown to most.

The cross. It is such a common thing. It is so faithful that it never misses its appointment every day. To take up this cross is all we need to make us saints.

The cross, the badge of the Christian, is unwanted by the world because it believes that by fleeing it, suffering can be escaped. The world does not know that the cross opens wide the soul of the person who has understood it to the kingdom of Light and of Love: that Love which the world seeks so much, but does not have.

Our Mother is so beautiful

O ur Mother is so beautiful in her contin-uous recollection as shown us by the Gospel: 'But Mary kept all these things, pon-dering them in her heart'. (Luke 2:19.)

That full silence fascinates the soul who loves.

How can I live like Mary in her mystical silence when our vocation at times is to talk in order to evangelize, always exposed in every kind of place, rich and poor, from cellars to streets, to schools, everywhere?

Our Mother also spoke: *she gave us Jesus*. There has never been a greater apostle in the world. No one ever spoke such words as she, who gave us the *Word*.

Our Mother is truly and deservedly called the Queen of the Apostles.

And she was silent. She was silent because the two could not speak at once. The word must always rest against a silence, like a paint-ing against a background.

She was silent because she was a creature. For nothingness does not speak. But upon that nothingness Jesus spoke and said: himself.

God, Creator and All, spoke upon the nothingness of the creature.

How then can I live Mary, how can my life be perfumed by her beauty?

By silencing the creature in me, and upon this silence letting the Spirit of the Lord speak.

In this way I live Mary and I live Jesus. I live Jesus upon Mary. I live Jesus by living Mary.

Enlarge our heart

We need to enlarge our heart to the measure of the heart of Jesus. How much work that means! Yet this is the only thing necessary. When this is done, all is done. It means loving everyone we meet as *God* loves them. And since we live in time, we must love our neighbours *one by one*, without holding in our heart any lingering affection for the brother or sister met a moment before. It is the same Jesus, after all, whom we love in everyone. If any lingering affection remains, it means that the preceding brother or sister was loved for our sake or for theirs . . . not for Jesus. That is the problem.

Our most important task is to maintain the chastity of God and that is: to keep love in our hearts as Jesus loves. Hence, to be pure we need not deprive our heart and repress the love in it. We need to enlarge our heart to the measure of the heart of Jesus and love everyone. And as one sacred host, from among the millions of hosts on the earth, is enough to nourish us with God, so one brother or sister, the one whom God's will puts next to us, is enough to give us communion with humanity, which is the mystical Jesus.

To have communion with our brother or sister is the second commandment, the one that comes immediately after the love of God, and is the expression of it.

Give me all who are lonely

Lord, give me all who are lonely . . . I have felt in my heart the passion that fills your heart for all of the forsakenness in which the whole of the world is drifting.

I love everyone who is sick and alone.

Who consoles their weeping?

Who mourns their slow death?

Who presses to their own heart, the heart in despair?

My God, let me be in this world the tangible sacrament of your love; let me be your arms that press to themselves and consume in love all the loneliness of the world.

Two secret things

Two things I ought to keep secret: love and suffering. For love is the love with which he loves me, or loves himself in me, and suffering is the love with which I love him.

The light, however, should be given.

Not mine but yours be done

'Not my will, but yours, be done'. (Luke 22:42.)

Strive to remain in his will and that his will should remain in you. When God's will is done on earth as in heaven, the testament of Jesus will be fulfilled.

Look at the sun and its rays.

The sun is the symbol of the divine will, which is God himself. The rays are the divine will for each of us.

Walk towards the sun in the light of your ray which is different and distinct from every other one, and fulfill the particular, wonderful plan that God wants from you.

There is an infinite number of rays, coming from the same sun . . . a single will, particular for each person.

The closer the rays get to the sun, the nearer they draw to one another. We too, the closer we get to God, by carrying out the divine will more and more perfectly, the nearer we draw to one another.

Until we are all one.

Jesus did not remain on earth

Jesus did not remain on earth, so that he could remain in all points of the earth in the Eucharist. He was God, and as a divine seed, he bore fruit, multiplying himself.

In the same way, we must die in order to multiply.

They do not pass

'It is easier for a camel to pass through the eye of a needle than for a rich man to enter the kingdom of God'. (Matt. 19:24.) The rich man who does not act as Jesus wants, gambles with eternity. Yet all of us are rich, until such time as Jesus lives in us in all his fullness.

Even the poor man who carries a chunk of bread in his bag and curses if anyone touches it, is as rich as others. His heart is attached to something that is not God. Unless he becomes poor, poor in the Gospel sense, he cannot enter the kingdom of heaven.

The way there is narrow and only that which is nothing can get past.

There are those who are rich in knowledge, and being puffed up by this impedes their passage into the kingdom and the passage of the kingdom into them, so that the Spirit of God's Wisdom finds no room in their soul.

There are those who are rich in presumption, arrogance, or human affections, and until they cut themselves off from everything, they are not with God. All things must be removed from the heart so as to put God there and all of creation according to God's order.

There are those who are rich in worries and do not know how to unload them into the heart of God, and live in torment. They do not have the joy and the peace and the charity that belong to the kingdom of heaven.

They do not pass.

There are those who are rich in their own sins, weeping over them and torturing themselves, instead of burning them in God's mercy and looking ahead, loving God and their neighbour, to make up for the time when they did not love.

We would die

We would die if we did not look at you, who transformed, as if by magic, every bitterness into sweetness; at you, crying out on the cross, in the greatest suspense, in total inactivity, in a living death, when, sunk in the cold, you hurled your fire upon the earth, and reduced to infinite immobility, you cast your infinite life to us, who now live it in rapture.

It is enough for us to see that we are like you, at least a little, and unite our suffering to yours and offer it to the Father.

So that we might have Light, you ceased to see.

So that we might have union, you experienced separation from the Father.

So that we might possess wisdom, you made yourself 'ignorance'.

So that we might be clothed with innocence, you made yourself 'sin'.

So that God might be in us, you felt him far from you.

The cold

C old freezes, but if excessive, it burns and chaps. Wine strengthens, but if too much, it saps your strength. Motion is as it is, but if it spins at its greatest speed, it appears still. The Spirit of God gives life, but if there is much of it . . . it inebriates. Jesus is love because he is God; but his great love for us made him cry out: 'My God, my God, why have you forsaken me?' (Matt. 27:46) and in this cry he appears merely a man.

Eloi, Eloi lama sabachthani?

'Eloi, Eloi lama sabachthani?' (Mark 15:34). These are the words that Jesus, in his forsakenness, cried out in the language of Mary, his mother.

'How meaningful is that cry of yours in the language of your mother! . . . When suffering reaches the limit where life itself is suspended . . . then if a shred of voice remains, we call our mother, because our mother is love.

'But you, being the Son of God, had all your love in God and to God you called out. And, as man, you also had love in your blessed mother; so that, in the impossibility of calling upon both, you called to the Father with the voice of your mother.

'How beautiful you are in that infinite suffering, Jesus forsaken!'

I wish to bear witness

I wish to bear witness before the world that Jesus forsaken has filled every void, illuminated every darkness, accompanied every solitude, annulled every suffering, cancelled every sin.

' I know only Christ and Christ crucified'

I have only one Spouse on earth:
Jesus crucified and forsaken.
I have no other God but him.
In him there is the whole of paradise with the
      Trinity
and the whole of the earth with Humanity.
Therefore what is *his* is mine, and nothing else.
And *his* is universal suffering, and therefore
      mine.
I will go through the world seeking it
in every instant of my life.
What hurts me is *mine*.
Mine the suffering that grazes me in the present.
Mine the suffering of the souls beside me.
Mine all that is not peace, not joy,
not beautiful, not lovable, not serene . . .
So it will be for the years I have left:
athirst for suffering, anguish, despair,
separation, exile, forsakenness, torment,
for . . . all that is him
and he is Suffering.

In this way I will dry up the waters of tribu-
    lation in many hearts nearby,
and through communion with my almighty
    Spouse,
in many faraway.
I shall pass as a fire
that consumes all that must fall
and leaves standing only the truth.

Watch

'Watch therefore . . . ' (Matt. 24:42.) The Gospel speaks of watching with our loins girt and a lighted candle in our hand, and it promises the watchful servant that, on his arrival, the master will gird himself and serve him.

Only love is watchful. To watch is characteristic of love. When we love a person, our heart always watches and waits for them, and every moment away from them is lived for them and is spent on the watch. Jesus wants love: so he asks us to watch.

If we are afraid, we are also watchful. Indeed, Jesus speaks of thieves . . .

We watch because we fear, and we fear because we love someone that we do not wish to lose.

Jesus demands love, but since he loves as well, he arouses fear if only he can save us. He acts like a mother who promises her children a reward or a punishment according to how they behave.

Jesus does not ask just for pure love, which gives without thinking about being repaid.

If only to see us saved, he also offers us reward and punishment.

His mass and ours

If you suffer and your suffering is such
that it prevents any activity,
remember the mass.
Jesus in the mass,
today as once before,
does not work, does not preach:
Jesus sacrifices himself out of love.
In life
we can do many things, say many words,
but the voice of suffering,
maybe unheard and unknown to others,
is the most powerful word,
the one that pierces heaven.
If you suffer,
immerse your pain in his:
say your mass;
and if the world does not understand
do not worry:
all that matters
is that you are understood by Jesus, Mary, the
saints.
Live with them,

and let your blood flow
for the good of humanity –
like him!
The mass!
It is too great to understand!
His mass, our mass.

The words of a father

The words of a father are always precious, since we must believe someone who speaks out of love. But when a father utters his final words before leaving this earth, they remain clearly imprinted on the minds of his children. They have as much value as all his other words put together. They are his last will.

A father's love is nothing when compared with the love of God.

The God become human, Jesus, also spoke and left us a will: 'May they all be one'. (John 17:21.)

Whoever directs his life towards unity, has understood the heart of God.

In this world we are all brothers and sisters and yet we pass each other as if we were strangers. And this happens even among baptized Christians.

The Communion of Saints, the Mystical Body exists. But this Body is like a network of darkened tunnels.

The power to illuminate them exists; in many individuals there is the life of grace, but Jesus did not only want this when he turned to the Father, invoking him. He wanted the unity of all human beings with God and with one another; he wanted the network of tunnels to be illuminated. He wanted Jesus to be present in every relationship with others, besides being in each soul.

This is his last will and testament, the most precious desire of God who gave his life for us.

If we are united, Jesus is among us

If we are united, Jesus is among us. And this has value. It is worth more than any other treasure that our heart may possess; more than mother, father, brothers, sisters, children. It is worth more than our house, our work, or our property; more than the works of art in a great city like Rome; more than our business deals; more than nature which surrounds us with flowers and fields, the sea and the stars; more than our soul.

It is he who, inspiring his saints with his eternal truths, leaves his mark upon every age.

This too is his hour. Not so much the hour of a saint but of him, of *him among us*, of him living in us as we build up – in the unity of love – his Mystical Body.

But we must enlarge Christ, make him grow in other members, become like him bearers of Fire.

Make one of all and in all the One.

It is then that we live the life that he gives us, moment by moment, in charity.

The basic commandment is brotherly love. Everything is of value if it expresses sincere, fraternal charity. Nothing we do is of value, if there is not the feeling of love for our brothers and sisters in it. For God is a Father and in his heart he has always and only his children.

In love what counts is to love

I n love what counts is to love. This is what it is like here on earth. Love (I speak of supernatural love which does not exclude natural love) is both so simple and so complex. It demands that you do your share and awaits the other's.

If you try to live only for love, you will realize that here on earth it is worthwhile doing your share. You do not know whether the other will ever come; and it is not necessary that it should. At times you will be disappointed, but you will never be discouraged if you convince yourself that in love what counts is to love.

And you love Jesus in your neighbour, Jesus who always returns to you, maybe in other ways.

He it is who steels your soul against the storms of the world and who melts it in love for all those who are around you, provided you remember that in love what counts is to love.

There are those who do things for love

T here are those who do things 'for love'. There are those who do things trying 'to be Love'. Someone who does things 'for love' may do them well, but, thinking he is doing a great service for his neighbour, who is sick for instance, he may annoy him with his chatter, his advice and with his help. Such charity is burdensome and not to the point.

Poor fellow! He may gain merit, but the other person gains a burden.

This is why we must 'be Love'.

Our destiny is like that of the planets: if they revolve, they are; if they do not, they are not. We are, in the sense that the life of God, not our life, lives in us, if we do not stop loving for one moment.

Love places us in God and God is Love.

But Love, which is God, is light and with the light we see whether our way of approaching and serving our neighbour is according to the heart of God, as our neighbour would wish it to be, as he would dream of it being, if he had beside him not us, but Jesus.

Whoever does not renounce

'Whoever of you does not renounce all that he has cannot be my disciple.' (Luke 14:33.)

'Whoever'. The words of Jesus are addressed to all Christians.

'All'. This is required of all who wish to be Christians. We may not be attached even to our soul (which is one of our possessions), but we must be detached from everything.

And here Jesus forsaken is the universal teacher.

The wise and the foolish virgins

The wise and the foolish virgins.
The oil is love.

Whoever has love is virgin, so, looking at things as God sees them, Mary Magdalen is more a virgin than many virgins who are proud of their virginity or who just do not love.

Jesus cannot know them, for Love knows only Love. The Bridegroom recognizes as his bride she who bears his name, something of himself, almost himself transferred into her, one with him.

Now God *is* Charity; nothing is more his than charity, since it is his essence.

God is powerful;
he is the Omnipotent

God is powerful; he is the Omnipotent. Mary has been called the 'omnipotent through grace'. She too is powerful: she can and she obtains. We are utter wretches. And those of us who believe they are different, are by this very fact the same as the rest of us.

But perhaps our impotence and our poverty – if we love God – can be of use to us. It can help us obtain something.

If our Father in heaven has willed Jesus to be our brother, and if he has prepared an immaculate creature in the human race for his coming, it is because we are in a bad state, with wounded souls, sinners.

Sin is to be hated. But the coming of Jesus on earth, understood properly, could make us die of joy, if God did not sustain us.

Jesus on earth ... who has become our brother ... who says: 'If you ask anything of the Father, he will give it to you in my name' (John 16:23), just as a well-behaved boy in a family would say to his wild brother who has moved him to pity: 'Go and ask father what you want and tell him I sent you', because he is sure that this will ensure him a better hearing.

Jesus on earth ... Jesus our brother ... Jesus who dies between thieves for us: he, the Son of God, sharing a common life with others.

Perhaps we too have a certain power over the heart of the Father, if we go to him as we are: wretched creatures who may well have done every possible wrong, but who, having repented and returned to his love, then say: 'After all, if you came among us, it was our weakness that attracted you, our wretchedness that moved you to compassion.'

Certainly, no earthly mother or father waits more anxiously for their lost child or does more to bring him back, than does our Father in heaven.

False prudence

What ruins some souls is a false 'prudence', as they call it. It is a human prudence that crops up whenever the divine appears. It looks like a virtue, but it is more repulsive than vice. It does not wish to upset anyone. It lets the rich go to hell ('for they have their reward already' [Luke 6:24]) because it gives them no light. Who knows what might happen! It lets the members of the family next door beat and even kill each other, because they could say that you should mind your own business or you might even be called to court as a witness. And what a nuisance that would be! It advises saints to be moderate because something might happen to them.

This prudence isolates itself and it isolates others, like the grip of a vice, because it is born of fear.

Most of all, it is upset with God because if he were to be too active in the world through his faithful children, he could cause a revolution, and those children, like Christ, might pay for it with their lives, since they are hated by the world as he was hated.

It is a counterfeit quality which, I believe, is promoted and encouraged by the devil, who can do much of his work in this atmosphere.

There was one man who never had it: Jesus Christ. When he began his public preaching, at his very first lesson, they immediately wanted to kill him. 'But passing through the midst of them he went away.' (Luke 4:30.)

If we look at his life with the eyes of these prudent people, we would call it all imprudence. Not only that: for if these prudent people were logical in their reasoning, they would reach the conclusion that his death, the cross, was his own fault . . . because of his imprudence.

I think there is not a single word of Jesus that does not clash with these people. For God and the world are completely opposite, and only those who know how to rise above the world, in order to follow in Christ's footsteps, can offer some hope to humanity.

I want to see her again in you

I went into church one day,
and with my heart full of trust, I asked:
'Why did you wish to remain on earth,
on every point of the earth,
in the most sweet Eucharist,
and you have not found
– you who are God –
also a way to bring and to leave here
Mary, the mother of all of us who journey?'
In the silence he seemed to reply:
'I have not left her because I want to see her
    again in you.
Even if you are not immaculate,
my love will virginize you,
and you, all of you,
will open your arms and hearts as mothers of
    humanity,
which, as in times past, thirsts for God
and for his mother.
It is you who now
must soothe pains, soothe wounds
dry tears.

Sing her litanies
and strive to mirror yourself in them'.

I was sick

In a hospital ward I once saw a man with a plaster cast. His chest and right arm were immobilized. With his left hand he tried to do everything . . . as best he could. The cast was a torture, but the left arm, although it was more tired than usual by the end of the day, grew stronger by doing twice its normal work.

We are members of one another and mutual service is *our duty*. Jesus did not merely advise us to serve one another, *he commanded us to do so*.

When we help someone out of charity, let us not believe we are saints. If our neighbour is powerless, we must help him and help him as he would help himself if he could. Otherwise, what kind of Christians are we?

If, later, our hour has come, and we need our neighbour's charity, let us not feel humiliated.

At the last judgement we shall hear Jesus repeat the words: 'I was sick and you visited me . . . ' (Matt. 25:36) I was in prison, I was naked, I was hungry . . . Jesus loves to hide himself precisely beneath the suffering and needy.

Therefore in these times too, let us be conscious of our dignity, and with our whole heart thank the person who helps us. But let us reserve the deepest gratitude for God who created the human heart to be charitable, and for Christ who, by proclaiming with his blood the Good News, and especially 'his' commandment, has spurred on countless hearts to help one another.

With this commandment Jesus has distinguished Christians of all centuries from others who have not yet entered his Church. If we Christians do not manifest this characteristic, we come to be confused with the world and lose the honour of being deemed 'children of God'. And – foolishly – we leave unused a weapon, perhaps the most powerful of all, for witnessing to God in an environment frozen by atheism, that paganizes everything, is indifferent and superstitious.

May the astonished world gaze at the display of brotherly harmony and say of us, as of those who gloriously went before us: 'See how they love one another'.

The lives of the saints

T he lives of the saints are identical even though they vary greatly. Once they have given themselves to God, he takes them under his special care, and as supreme artist and supreme Love, he makes them into divine masterpieces. Angelic spirits or the eyes of other saints can understand them, or the insight, illuminated by a singular grace, of those in the Church who have to give judgment concerning them. To others, for the most part, their intimate selves are hidden and incomprehensible, because in the saint God lives more than man, and only the pure of heart see God.

The saint's life is made up of abysses and peaks: bottomless abysses, nights black as hell, dark tunnels where the soul, invaded by an absolutely superior light, is dazzled in a dark contemplation and submerged in a sea of anguish or near desperation due to its clear awareness of its own nothingness and wretchedness. The saint lives through months, years, during which his only yearning is to die into the the bosom of God, from whom at times he feels hopelessly separated. Life is an atrocious death and sleep a relief, a respite, almost a caress for the wounded soul. A long time passes in which the saint cries out, calling for pardon, for salvation, with no longer anything in his heart but God, his God . . .

Then, after a long time of being worked upon in a crucible comparable to purgatory, the soul of the saint is slowly drawn by its divine Craftsman into a life that is serene, full, radiant, active and immune to any blow. But *now* in the soul it is no longer itself that lives. In it glorious and strong, honoured and heeded, there lives the Creator and Lord of every human heart.

This is the hour when an unknown, unique, divine strength flourishes in the saint which fuses together the most contrasting virtues in his soul: meekness and strength, mercy and justice, simplicity and prudence. He rejoices in his life in God and offers to his Lord 'sacrifices of joy' (Ps. 27:6) with a joy that the world does not know. He is forced to admit that no dream is comparable to the Life he possesses, a Life which is divine and extraordinary (because it is a life of love), full of harmony and fruits.

Then God uses him for his great works that make up and adorn the heavenly city, the Church, which is destined to ascend to God as the spotless and worthy *Bride of Christ* who founded it.

Human beings are only given one life. It would be in the interest of each one to place his life in the hands of God who gave it. This, in a rational and free person, would be the highest possible act of intelligence, the most effective way of maintaining and extending his own freedom to a divine level. It would mean the deification of his own poor self in the name of the One who said: 'You are gods, sons of the Most High, all of you.' (Ps. 82:6.)

Time is fast escaping me

Time is fast escaping me;
  accept, O Lord, my life!
In my heart I hold you, the treasure
that must shape every move I make.
Follow me, watch over me, yours
is my loving: rejoicing and suffering.
May no one catch even a sigh.
Hidden in your tabernacle
I live, I work for all.
May the touch of my hand be yours,
only yours be the tone of my voice.
In this rag of myself
may your Love return to this arid world,
with the water that gushes abundantly
from your wound, O Lord.
Let Wisdom divine
clear away the gloomy affliction of many,
of all. In this may Mary shine out.

Before going up
to Calvary

Before going up to Calvary, during what were probably the most intimate hours that Jesus spent with his apostles, at the last supper he called them: 'children'. (John 13:33.) Indeed, one translation has it as: 'My little children'. He had become man for them, and now he was about to shed his blood in the way he did, for their salvation. With good reason he could call them 'children'.

Then he died on the cross, and three days later he appeared to the weeping Magdalen and said: 'Go to my brothers and say to them, I am ascending to my Father and your Father, to my God and your God.' (John 20:17.)

It is true and divine love, incarnate love in Jesus, that makes him say 'children', not only to the disciples who are present, but also, through them, to all those who were to follow him. But he shows himself to be even more love, when he says to Magdalen: 'Go to my brothers'.

It is fairly easy to think of God as Father, since a father always has a superiority that distinguishes him from his child.

But to think of God as our brother, who together with us in heaven adores his Father and ours, is such a great mystery that we can only begin to perceive it if we bear in mind that God is truly Love. Love which, having deserved, as Man, every title of fatherhood towards the human race (for whom he became incarnate, lived and died), at the end of his earthly life puts himself alongside those others whom he has reunited with the Father, made partakers of his divinity, and made by his Love like him. They say indeed that love makes the beloved resemble the lover, and this can be seen in Jesus with unique clarity.

What characterizes Jesus the Saviour, then, is that he addresses those brotherly words to a woman who had been a sinner. He used precisely her to give his message to the apostles, those who formed his newly born Church. The purpose of the incarnation and passion of Christ was the salvation of what was lost.

And Jesus always aims at this and is never untrue to himself.

The Church, too, was founded in order to continue this mission. Hence Jesus conveyed the most extraordinary message, the news of the most sublime miracle, to his elect through Mary Magdalen. That death had been particularly for her, for sinners who had been purified and made worthy by the love and the blood of Jesus, made worthy even to the point of announcing to those who, by vocation, would have to transmit to the world the great message of Jesus' resurrection, and of the resurrection through him and with him of all those who love him.

If a city were set on fire

I f a city were set on fire at different points, even by a small fire, but one that resisted being put out, in a short while the city would be aflame. If a city, in the most diverse points, were set on fire by the one that Jesus brought to earth and, through the goodwill of the inhabitants, that fire resisted the ice of the world, we would soon have the city aflame with the love of God.

The fire that Jesus brought to earth is himself. It is charity: that love which not only binds the soul to God, but also souls to one another.

In fact, a lighted supernatural fire means the continual triumph of God in souls who have given themselves to him and, because they are united to him, united among themselves.

Two or more people united in the name of Christ, who are not afraid or ashamed to declare explicitly to one another their desire to love God, but who actually make of this unity in Christ their Ideal, are a divine power in the world.

And in every city these souls can come to exist in families: father and mother, son and father, mother and mother-in-law. They can meet in parishes, in associations, in social bodies, in schools, in offices, everywhere.

It is not necessary for them to be saints already, or Jesus would have said so. It is enough for them to be united in the name of Christ and that they never go back on this unity.

Naturally, they will not remain two or three for very long, for charity spreads of itself and grows by enormous proportions.

Every small cell, set alight by God in any point of the earth, will necessarily spread, and Providence will distribute these flames, these souls on fire, wherever it thinks fit, so that the world in many places may be restored to the warmth of the love of God, and hope again.

But there is a secret by which this lighted cell may grow and become a tissue and give life to the parts of the Mystical Body. It is that those who make up the Body should throw themselves into the Christian adventure, which means *making a spring-board of every obstacle*. They should not just 'put up' with the cross in whatever guise it presents itself, but should wait for it and embrace it, minute by minute, as the saints do.

It is a matter of saying, whenever the cross comes: 'This is what I wanted, Lord! I know I belong to the Church Militant, where we have to struggle. I know the Church Triumphant awaits me, where I shall see you for all eternity. While I am still here on earth, I prefer suffering to everything else, because with your life you have told me that only in suffering is there true value.'

And having said 'yes' to the Lord, the soul must live fully the moment that follows, not thinking of itself, of its own pain. But it must think of the suffering of others, or of the joys of others that it must share, or the burdens of others that it must bear with them. Or it must think of the fulfilment of its duties to which, because God wills it and in order to lift them up as a continuous prayer, it must give the attention of all its mind, the affection of all its heart and all the vigour of its strength.

This is the little secret with which, brick by brick, we build up the city of God within us and among us. And already on this earth, it places us within the divine will, which is God, the eternal present.

When we have known suffering

When we have known suffering in all shades of its most frightful forms, in the most varied kinds of anguish, and have stretched out our arms to God in mute, heart-rending supplication, uttering subdued cries for help; when we have drunk the chalice to the dregs and have offered to God, for days and years, our own cross mingled with his, which gives it divine value, then God has pity on us and welcomes us into union with him.

This is the moment in which, having experienced the unique value of suffering, having believed in the economy of the cross and seen its beneficial effects, God shows us in a new and higher way something that is worth even more than suffering. *It is love for others in the form of mercy*, the love that stretches our hearts and arms to embrace the wretched, the poor, those whom life has ravaged, repentant sinners.

A love that knows how to welcome back our neighbour who went astray, our friend, our brother or a stranger, and pardons him an infinite number of times. It is a love that rejoices more over one sinner who comes back than over a thousand of the just, and that puts intelligence and possessions at the service of God, so as to enable him to show the prodigal son the happiness caused by his return.

It is a love that does not measure and will not be measured.

It is charity in bloom, which is more abundant, more universal, more down to earth than the charity the soul had before. Indeed, it senses within itself the birth of feelings similar to those of Jesus, and it notices coming to its lips with reference to all those it meets, the divine words: 'I have compassion on the crowd.' (Matt. 15:32.) It starts conversations with sinners who draw near, because it has a certain likeness to Christ, such as those conversations Jesus once had with Mary Magdalen, with the Samaritan woman, or with the adulteress.

Mercy is the ultimate expression of charity, and is that which fulfils it. Charity surpasses suffering, for suffering belongs to this life alone, whereas love continues also to the next. God prefers mercy to sacrifice.

Inconceivable

Inconceivable, extraordinary,
something that cuts an ever deeper
    impression on my soul
is your stillness there,
in silence, in the tabernacle.
I come to church in the morning, and I find
    you there.
I run to church when I love you,
and I find you there.
I drop in by chance or habit or respect,
and I find you there.
And each time
you say a word to me
or you rectify a feeling.
In reality you are composing from different
    notes a single song,
a song that my heart has learnt by heart
and that repeats to me one word alone:
eternal love.
Oh! God, you could not invent anything
    better!
That silence of yours

in which the din of our life is hushed,
that silent heartbeat
which absorbs every tear;
that silence . . .
that silence, more sonorous than the song of
     angels;
that silence
which communicates the Word to the mind
and gives the divine balm to the heart;
that silence
in which every voice finds itself channelled
and every prayer feels transformed;
That mysterious presence of yours . . .
Life is there,
expectation is there;
there our little heart rests
before continuing, without pause,
on its way.

A myriad of splendid pearls

I picture a city of gold,
   where the divine stands out in relief,
      resplendent with light,
and the human forms its background,
having withdrawn into the shade,
to give greater stress to the splendour.
Every church, every tabernacle,
glows more brightly than the sun,
because in them has remained
the Love of loves.
In the soul of those who represent the Church,
in the hierarchy that gives structure to the
      divine society,
brought down on earth from heaven,
I find a myriad of splendid pearls:
they are the graces deposited by God,
through the hands of the Virgin,
in that channel, which has the one purpose
of quenching my thirst for light,
and of nourishing me with honey from heaven,
as a more than heavenly mother who feeds her
      child.

And if, recollected in God,
I open the book of life and read the eternal
      Words,
I hear a harmony full of light
sing in my soul,
and the Spirit of God shines through me with
      his gifts.
When I meet anyone,
noble or wretched,
I see each face transfigured
into the most beautiful face
of the Word incarnate,
Light from Light.
When I go into the homes of people who love
      one another, or families united in Christ,
I see a divine reflection of the Trinity,
and I hear expressed by the community,
the Word that is life:
God.
God is the gold of my city,
before whom the sun itself is dimmed,
the sky dwindles,
all the beauty and majesty of nature
recedes, happy to encircle, to serve,
simply a frame.

And this city is in every city
and everyone may see it,
provided that our soul extinguishes itself in
    God,
forgetting itself,
and lit in it is the fire of love divine.

The little seed

Have you ever seen
how on a disused road,
when it is caressed by the spring,
grass grows up and life, incessantly, flowers
    again?
The same thing happens to humanity around
    you
if you neglect seeing it with an earthly eye
and restore it with the divine ray of charity.
Supernatural love in your soul
is a sun,
which allows no respite in the reflowering of
    life.
It is a life
that makes your corner of life a corner-stone.
Nothing else is needed to uplift the world,
to give it back to God.
Beauty of speech, delicacy of manner,
the weight of culture, the experience of years,
are certainly gifts that should not be neglected.
But for the eternal kingdom
that which has most life has most value.

The sweet-scented slice of an apple
is good to see, tasty, pleasant, and colourful,
but, underground, it dies and leaves no trace.
A little seed, unpleasant to the palate,
tasteless and insipid,
underground, yields new apples.
So it is with life in God, the life of a Christian,
the fiery progress of the Church.
The Church stands, erect and majestic, upon
    pillars
that the centuries have called senseless and
    foolish and mad . . .
against which the prince of the world has
    hurled his fury
in order to destroy them down to their final
    offshoot.
They have remained.
The Father cleansed them
so that joined to the vine they might bear
    abundant fruit
and he raised them up in glory
in the kingdom of life.
You and I, the milkman, the farmer, the porter,
the fisherman, the labourer, the newsboy . . .
And all the others,

disillusioned idealists, mothers weighed down
    with worries,
lovers near their wedding day,
exhausted old ladies waiting for death,
boys bursting with energy, all . . .
All are raw material
for God's society:
it is enough that they have a heart that holds
    high and upright,
fixed in God,
the flame of love.

Thrust towards the infinite

The saints are great men and women
who, having seen their greatness in the
Lord,
risk for God, as his children,
everything that is theirs.
They give, demanding nothing.
They give their life, their soul, their joy,
every earthly bond, every richness.
Free and alone
thrust towards the infinite,
they wait for Love to bring them
into the eternal kingdom; but, already in this
life,
they feel their hearts fill with love,
true love, the only love
that satisfies, that consoles,
that love which shatters
the eyelids of the soul and gives
new tears.
Ah, no one knows who a saint is!
He has given and now he receives,
and an endless flow

passes between heaven and earth,
joins earth to heaven,
and filters from the depths
rare ecstasy, celestial sap
that does not stop at the saint,
but flows over the tired, the mortal,
the blind and paralysed in soul,
and breaks through and refreshes,
comforts and attracts and saves.
If you want to know about love, ask a saint.

I have found you

I have found you in so many places, Lord!
I have felt you throbbing
in the perfect stillness
of a little Alpine church,
in the shadow of the tabernacle
of an empty cathedral,
in the breathing as one soul
of a crowd who love you and who fill
the arches of your church
with songs and love.
I have found you in joy.
I have spoken to you
beyond the starry firmament,
when in the evening, in silence,
I was returning home from work.
I seek you and often I find you.
But where I *always* find you
is in suffering.
A suffering, any sort of suffering,
is like the sound of a bell
that summons God's bride to prayer.

When the shadow of the cross appears
the soul recollects itself
in the tabernacle of its heart
and forgetting the tinkling of the bell
it 'sees' you and speaks to you.
It is you who come to visit me.
It is I who answer you:
'Here I am, Lord, I desire you, I have desired
        you.'
And in this meeting
my soul does not feel its suffering,
but is as if inebriated with your love:
suffused with you, imbued with you:
I in you and you in me,
that we may be one.
And then I reopen my eyes to life,
to the life less real,
divinely trained
to wage your war.

There is no thorn without a rose

How sad to think that the lives of many people are simply not lived! They do not live because they do not see. They do not see because they look at the world, at things, at their relatives, at people, with their own eyes. Whereas to see it would be enough to follow every event, every thing, every person with the eyes of God. We see if we place ourselves in God and know him as Love, if we believe in his love and think like the saints that 'everything that God wills or permits is for my sanctification'.

Joy and grief, birth and death, anguish and exultation, failure and triumph, encounters, acquaintances, work, sickness, unemployment, wars and disasters, a child's smile, a mother's love, everything is the raw material for our sanctity.

Around our being moves a world of all sorts of values: a divine world, an angelic world, a world of brotherhood, a lovable world and a hostile world, which have all been prepared by God for our divinization, which is our true end.

In this world everyone is a centre, because the law of everything is love.

And if because of the human and divine balance of our life, and by will of the Most High, we must love, always love the Lord and our brothers and sisters, then the will of God, what God allows, and other beings – whether they know it or not – serve us, act out their existence, for love of us. Indeed for those who love, all things work together for good.

With our darkened and unbelieving eyes, we often do not see how each and everyone has been created as a gift for us, and we as a gift for others.

But it is so. And a mysterious bond of love links persons and things, guides history, orders the destiny of peoples and of individuals, while respecting their freedom to the full.

But when the soul, which has abandoned itself to God, has for some time made the law of 'believing in love' (cf. 1 John 4:16) its own, God shows himself. With newly opened eyes the soul sees that from every trial it gathers new fruit, every fight is followed by victory, every tear flowers in a smile that is new, always new, because God is Life, who allows torture, evil, for a greater good.

The soul understands that the life of Jesus does not culminate in the *via crucis* and in death, but in the resurrection and the ascension to heaven.

Then the human way of seeing things fades and becomes meaningless, and bitterness no longer poisons the brief joys of this earthly life. For the soul that proverb which is so full of melancholy, 'There is no rose without a thorn', means nothing. But because of the wave of the revolution of love into which God has drawn the soul, the exact opposite is true: 'There is no thorn without a rose'.

An invasion of love

T he world is made up of unhappy people because humanity has not grasped the source of its happiness. The star shines in the sky and the earth stays in existence because they move: motion is the life of the universe. The human being is fully happy only if he starts up, and keeps running, the motor of his life: love.

Even the person who calls himself happy because he has made a good marriage, because he has come into an inheritance, because he spends his life in luxury, sport, entertainment, sooner or later experiences voids within his soul – inevitably. The poor wretch, on the other hand, to whom everything seems to deny life, if he starts to love, possesses more than the rich man and enjoys on earth the fullness of the kingdom of heaven.

This is truth; it is a reality.

Humanity pines away in its search for peace, awaits, builds in order to reach enjoyment, but when the time comes, is dejected as it waits for death, which it wishes would never come.

The children of God are the children of love! They fight with a weapon that is the very life of the human race. Their battle is to bring back order to souls and society, so that souls may shine more than the stars, and society compose other, lasting constellations in the eternal pavilions of the God of the living.

If humanity were to see how God sees the human race, it would be horrified.

Because even the best, those who have raised themselves above the level of the majority through art or science, have only developed a part of the spirit, leaving the rest to atrophy.

Only love in a soul, only God in a soul can radiate splendour through it with balance in every part.

A soul that loves is a little sun in the world, passing on God. A soul that does not love, vegetates and has little of the Church, nothing of Mary and is the antithesis of Christ.

The world needs an invasion of love and this depends on each one of us. The human being is the reservoir of this precious element – the human being in the grace of God. Everyday countless numbers of people die, even the great, and little is left of them. But a saint passes to eternal Life, reawakening, when the Lord calls him, to the identical though changed life he lived before, and everyone speaks of him. And the memory of him is handed down from generation to generation, and his example is followed by many. On that bed where lies his body but not his soul, no one manages to understand death, but all realize what Life is. Love does not die and, because it serves, it makes those who love into kings.

If a soul gives itself to God sincerely

I f a soul gives itself to God sincerely; he works on it. And love and suffering are the raw materials of his divine game – suffering to dig abysses in the soul, love to soothe the suffering and still more love that fills the soul, giving it the equilibrium of peace.

The soul realizes that it is under the powerful hand of God and waits in silent suspense as it watches, despite its tears, the work of the Beloved.

But at times God works the soul to such a point that it is ground down in agonies sharper than death. It no longer feels the help or spiritual support of anyone. For it the whole earth has become an endless desert.

Then the new miracle is born: a boundless trust, a desperate confidence in God who, to prepare it for heaven, permits its sufferings and its nights. And between God and the soul begins a new dialogue, one known only to them. The soul says, 'Lord, you see how I am surrounded by the shadows of death. You are aware of the extreme uncertainty of my spirit, and you know that no one seems able to calm me. You take care of me. I trust in you. And while waiting to come to Life, I'll work for you, in the interests of heaven.'

The soul is like the bloom of a flower which has opened itself to the love of God and which, detached from its stem, rises in the sun, always closer to its light and its heat. Until, in the hour that God has established, the two merge and it is no longer uncertain, no longer alone, but peaceful now forever in the infinite sea of peace which is God.

The saint's masterpiece

O ften, going into the parlour of a monastic house, whether a recent or an ancient foundation, one sees the portrait of the founder, usually a saint, with the Rule in hand.

Someone from the world goes in, looks and does not understand – or understands little.

A saint earns the affection of most people, also of non-Christians or even of atheists. But people like to imagine him either in the ecstasy of contemplation or mingling with those whom he benefits; or in the stories that pass from mouth to mouth and which almost always surround the figure of a saint. Sometimes these are minute events that have been eternalized in time by a phrase, a gesture, which no one else would have said or done except that saint. For guided by God, his gesture keenly shows the unmistakable meeting between the divine and the human, which gives a new, and at times revolutionary, note to the boring and always monotonous life of the world.

But the saint who is a founder is not only this.

The founder is a human being who has done what God wanted, who has made the effort (with an ever more total and generous gift of self to God) to be perfect like the Father.

In reality the saint is a little father or a little mother because God is Love, and to be full of God is to become sharers in the divine fertility of Love.

A founder can be understood if one looks at what he has done.

The saint's most important work is the small or large flock that has followed him, which he has ordered in a family, through the eternal laws of the Gospel made to ring out with a new and up-to-date power by the Holy Spirit in his spirit: it represents the same thing that for a mother is represented by her child, her very own child.

When the founder believes the work of God has been completed, then abandoned in God, as an instrument in the hands of an artist, he draws up the essential plan of the work and writes a Rule. He or she has to do this and wants to do it with the same strength with which a mother says, 'This is my child and no other.'

In her baby a mother is repaid for all her suffering and it is the liveliest reminder of the love that bound her to its father. It has its particular features, its own character, its own blood.

The saint loves God with a love as distant from human love as heaven is distant from the earth, and this love gives him small and immense sufferings, small and ineffable joys in the God of the beatitudes.

But joys and sufferings are not ends in themselves; they are the means by which the Church will have a new work of God. The Lord shapes it with a given form and unique characteristics, infusing it with a divine blood, which is the particular spirit that informs it and from which part of humanity in that age should benefit.

The Rule gives witness to, explains, establishes, preserves all this, and doing so, it is the saint's masterpiece.

Diplomacy

When someone weeps, we must weep with them. And if they laugh, rejoice with them. Thus the cross is divided and borne by many shoulders, and joy is multiplied and shared by many hearts.

To make ourselves one with our neighbour is the way, the main way, of making ourselves one with God – the main way because in this charity there is the fusion of the two first and most important commandments.

To make ourselves one with our neighbour for love of Jesus, with the love of Jesus, so that our neighbour, sweetly wounded by the love of God in us will want to make himself one with us, in a mutual exchange of help, of ideals, of projects, of affections. Do this until establishing between the two of us those essential elements for the Lord to say, 'Where two or three are gathered in my name, there am I in the midst of them.' (Matt. 18:20.) Until, that is, as far as it depends on us, the presence of Jesus is guaranteed, so that we walk through life, always, as a little Church on the move – Church whether we are at home, at school, in a garage or in Parliament.

To walk in life like the disciples of Emmaus with that Third among them, who gives divine value to all our actions.

Then we are not the ones acting in our life, we who are miserable and limited, lonely and suffering. The Almighty walks with us. And whoever remains united with him bears much fruit.

From one cell come more cells, from one tissue many tissues. Making ourselves one with our neighbour in that complete self forgetfulness which is possessed (without realizing it or specifically trying to do it) by someone who thinks of the other, their neighbour.

This is the diplomacy of charity, which has many of the expressions and aspects of ordinary diplomacy, hence it does not say all that it could say, for this would not be liked by others or be pleasing to God. It knows how to wait, how to speak, how to reach its goal. The divine diplomacy of the Word who becomes flesh to make us divine.

This diplomacy, however, has an essential and characteristic mark that differentiates it from the diplomacy spoken about by the world, for which to say diplomatic is often synonymous with reticence or even falsehood.

The divine diplomacy has this greatness and this property, perhaps a property of it alone: it is moved by the good of the other and is therefore devoid of any shadow of selfishness.

This rule of life ought to inform every kind of diplomacy, and with God it can be done because he is not only the master of individuals, but king of the nations and of every society.

If every diplomat in the exercise of his duty were inspired in his actions by charity towards the other State as to his own, he would be enlightened by the help of God to such an extent as to contribute to the establishment of relationships among States as they ought to exist among human beings. Charity is a light and a guide, and he who is sent as an emissary has all the graces to be a good emissary.

May God help us and may we co-operate, so that from heaven the Lord may see this new sight: his last will and testament brought to life among the nations.

It may seem like a dream to us, but for God it is the norm, the only one that guarantees peace in the world, the fulfilment of individuals in the unity of a humanity that by now knows Jesus.

Christ will be my cloister

I believe there is no man's heart, still less a woman's, that has not at least once, especially in youth, felt the attraction of the cloister.

It is not the attraction of a cloistered way of life, but of something that seems to be concentrated there, between those four walls, something that makes itself felt, resounding deeply, even from a distance.

In these communities, with which the world, thank God, is strewn like a dark night dotted with constellations, there is the light of the presence of God. A presence that stands out strongly, because it blossoms on the background of persons who, for God, have wished to immolate in the shadows their own poor appearance.

Though sunken in silence, these houses of brothers or sisters united in God, through the mysterious power of celestial things, speak to the hearts of human beings and utter a voice unknown to the world: a blessedness of union with God that humanity longs for.

Yet also my own home can have the perfume of the cloister; also the walls where I live can become a kingdom of peace, God's fortress in the midst of the world.

It is not so much the external din of the radio turned on at full blast by the tenant next door, or the roar of the traffic, or the yelling of the newspaper boys, that take away the enchantment from my house. It is rather every noise within me that makes where I live become an open square unprotected by walls, because unprotected by love.

The Lord is within me. He would like to move my actions, permeate my thoughts with his light, arouse my will, give me, in short, the law of my stillness and of my movement.

But there is my ego which, at times, does not let him live in me. If it stops interfering, God himself will take possession of all my being and he will know how to give these walls the importance of an abbey, and this room the sacredness of a church, my sitting at table the sweetness of liturgy, my clothes the perfume of a blessed habit, the sound of the doorbell or the telephone the joyous note of a meeting with my brothers and sisters, which interrupts, yet continues, my conversation with God.

Then, upon the silence of me, Another will speak and, upon my extinguishing myself, a light will be lit. And it will shine afar, passing beyond and almost consecrating these walls that protect a member of Christ, a temple of the Holy Spirit. And other people will come to my house to seek the Lord with me, and in our shared, loving search, the flame will grow, the divine melody will rise a tone. And my heart, though in the midst of the world, will ask for nothing more.

Christ will be my cloister, the Christ of my heart, Christ in the midst of our hearts.

The exam

I f you were a student and by chance came to know the questions of the school's end of year exams, you would consider yourself lucky and study the answers thoroughly.

Life is a trial and at the end it, too, has to pass an exam; but the infinite love of God has already told humanity what the questions will be: 'For I was hungry and you gave me food, I was thirsty and you gave me drink'. (Matt. 25:35.) The works of mercy will be the subject of the exam, those works in which God sees if you love him truly, having served him in your brothers and sisters.

Perhaps this is why the Pope, the vicar of Christ, often simplifies Christian life by underlining the works of mercy.

And we do the will of Jesus in heaven and of his Church on earth, if we transform our life into a continuous work of mercy. In fact, it is not difficult and does not make much of a change in what we are already doing. It is a matter of raising every relationship with our neighbour onto a supernatural plane. Whatever our vocation may be, fathers or mothers, farmers or office staff, Members of Parliament or Heads of State, students or workers, throughout the day there are continuous opportunities, directly or indirectly, to feed the hungry, instruct the ignorant, bear with those who annoy us, give advice to those in doubt, pray for the living and for the dead.

A new intention behind every move we make for the benefit of our neighbour, whoever it may be, and every day of our life will help us to prepare for the eternal day, storing up treasure where moth and rust do not corrupt.

You only use one tactic

I have noticed that you use only one tactic, but it is never monotonous, perhaps because your action is you, Lord. And you are Love that is always new. Your tactic is this: when a soul is content with shadows, and I do not mean mortal shadows, that is to say when its life is for you, but is not you, you often offer a suffering. Then the soul turns to you and says its 'yes'. But at times that 'yes' is perfumed with a sense of profound gratitude and immersed in a very special prayer: 'Yes, Lord, meeting the cross, I find you upon it. Thank you for having called me back to you, and not only to that which concerns you; because more than any other thing, what attracts me is solitude with you, that same solitude which I will be forced to face on the day of our meeting, if I do not choose it now with love. And you who can do everything, in your name make it possible for me to attain this continuous conversation between you in me and you, in which events, people and things are nothing but the fuel of our pure love.'

Only this is the true life, because it is a spark of you – a life without deceit, without disappointment, without pauses and with no decline.

How do you become a saint?

I t often happens that souls are attracted by the idea of sanctity. And perhaps it is the grace of God that is working upon them, stirring up such a desire.

The awareness of a saint's value, the influence of his personality upon his age, the widespread and continuous revolution he brings in the world, are often the things that spark off the flame of this yearning.

But at times the soul, delicately tormented by its desire, finds itself before the saints as before an insuperable chasm or an impregnable wall.

'How do you become a saint?' it asks itself.

'What is the measure, the system, the method, the way?'

'If I knew it were penance, I'd scourge myself all day. If I knew that prayer is required, I'd pray night and day. If it were enough to preach, I'd want to travel through towns and cities, giving myself no rest, to announce the word of God to all . . . but I don't know, I don't know the way.'

Every saint has his own features, and the

saints differ from one another as do the most varied flowers in a garden.

But perhaps there is a way: one good for everyone.

Maybe it is not necessary to look for our own path, or to make a plan, or to dream up programmes, but to plunge ourselves into the moment that passes and fulfil in that instant the will of the One who called himself 'the way' *par excellence* (John 14:6). The moment that has passed, is no longer; the coming one will perhaps never be in our possession. What is certain is that God can be loved in the present that is given to us.

Sanctity is built in time.

No one knows their own sanctity, or often that of others, while they are still alive. Only when the soul has run its course, has proved its worth, does it reveal to the world the plan God had for it.

All we have to do is to build our sanctity moment by moment, responding with all our heart, soul, strength, to the love God has for us, a personal love, as our heavenly Father, a full love, as great as the charity of a God.

Our responsibility is great

Certainly our responsibility is great, because we Christians must be witnesses of Christ and, from the way we behave, others can sense the nature of the message Jesus brought to earth.

But sometimes it happens that the witness we give of Christ is little or nothing, or is disfigured in one way or another.

A variety of characters and minds unresponsive to the action of grace give an idea of Jesus in their own image and likeness, hence the world, which sees and observes, deduces as much as it can deduce from the data it possesses: that religion, for example, bends people's necks, but not their will. For a particular Christian who says he is a disciple of Christ, yet with he who lives in himself and not Christ in him, casts a shadow that veils, in his person, the religion he professes. As a result, there continues, tragically perpetuated, the separation of those 'far away' from those who, living out

Love which is God, ought to attract the world and bring it to the Lord.

In short: a religion that is distasteful because distorted; while even the most agnostic of people have a fascination or at least a respect, albeit unexpressed, for the missionary who hazards remote shores, leaving everything for God, or for the martyr who consumes his life in blood.

And this, all of this, because Christianity is either genuine and total or it leaves much to find fault with.

All that has been said is obvious in many cases. But going to a higher, more subtle level, not infrequently when coming close to people who have given themselves with true enthusiasm to God, we meet with errors, perhaps of a practical nature, that are offensive and obscure the beauty of our faith.

At times our life's journey on this planet is so hard and this 'vale' so full of tears, that people, finding comfort only in the cross, cling to it, make it their banner, present it also to others, bring them to love it, but . . . they stop there. They stop there because, although they love with all their heart and love in deeds, *they do not believe enough in the love of God for them and for everyone*.

The mystery of Easter is there to testify that Jesus who conquers death is light that shatters the shadows, is fullness that annihilates the void.

In the final analysis this is Christianity, in which the cross is essential, but as a *means*, and tears are portents of consolation and poverty of the possession of the kingdom; in which purity opens the curtain on heaven, and persecution and meekness foretell the triumph of Eternity and guarantee the advance of the Church in the world.

Out of fifteen mysteries that bejewel the rosary, the Church sets out five as joyful, five as sorrowful, and five as glorious, and this makes it clear that the Christian should always hope, should sing, as the first Christians did, even on the threshold of martyrdom, because *our* heritage is the fullness of joy that Jesus

promised and invoked for those who were to
follow him.

Let us help one another, in our small way, to
be complete witnesses of that Jesus who has
attracted our hearts, in that Church which we
too can help to beautify, so that the pilgrim in
this world, seeing it, can say more easily and
with infinite relief, 'Yes, this is the true
Church.'

The only good

'God's will be done' is an expression that, for the most part, is said by Christians in moments of suffering, when there is no other way out; when faith, before the inevitable destruction of what one had thought, desired, wanted, surfaces again and one accepts what God has decreed. But it is not like this, solely, that God's will is to be done. In Christianity there is more than just 'Christian resignation'.

The Christian's life is a fact that has roots in heaven, as well as on earth.

The Christian, through his faith, can and must always be in touch with Another who knows his life and his destiny. And this Other is not of this earth, but of another world. And he is not a merciless judge or an absolute monarch who only asks for service. He is a Father. One, therefore, who is such because he is in relationship with others, and in this case with his children, children adopted through his only Son, who from all eternity dwells with him.

The Christian's life therefore is not and cannot be decided by his will or his own foresight alone. Unfortunately many Christians wake up in the morning full of the sadness and boredom the coming day will bring. They grumble about lots of things, past and future and present, because it is they themselves who make the plan for their lives. Such a plan, the fruit of human intelligence and a restricted forecast, cannot fully satisfy a human being, athirst for the infinite. They substitute themselves for God, at least so far as their own affairs are concerned, and like the prodigal son, having taken their inheritance, they squander it in their own way, without their father's advice, outside the life of their family.

We Christians are very often blind people who have abdicated our supernatural dignity, for we repeat, maybe every day, in the 'Our Father': 'Your will be done on earth as it is in heaven.' But we neither understand what we say, nor do we do (for our part at least) what we implore.

God sees and knows the course we must follow every instant of our lives. For each of us he has established a celestial orbit, in which the star of our freedom ought to turn, if it abandons itself to the One who created it. Our orbit, our life, does not conflict with other orbits or with the paths of other beings, children of the Father like us, but harmonizes with them in a firmament more splendid than that of the stars, because it is spiritual. God must move our life and draw it into a divine adventure, which is unknown to us; one in which, at the same time spectators and actors of the marvellous plans of love, we give moment by moment the contribution of our free will.

We can give! Not: we must give! Or worse: let us resign ourselves to giving!

He is the Father and therefore is Love. He is the Creator, our Redeemer, the Sanctifier. Who better than he knows what is good for us?

'Lord, may your will really be done, may it be done now and always! May it be done in me, in my children, in others, in their children, in the whole of humanity.

'Be patient and forgive our blindness, for we do not understand and we force heaven to remain closed and prevent it pouring its gifts upon the earth. For, by shutting our eyes, we say with the way we live that it is night and there is no heaven.

'Draw us into the ray of your light, of our light, decreed by your love when, out of love, you created us.

'And force us to kneel every minute in adoration of your will – the one good, pleasing, holy, rich, fascinating, fruitful will. Thus, when the hour of suffering arrives, we may also see your infinite love beyond it. And we may (being full of you) see with your eyes already on this earth and observe from above the divine pattern that you have woven for us and for our brothers and sisters, in which everything turns out to be a splendid design of love. And may our eyes be spared, at least a little, from seeing the knots lovingly tied by your mercy, tempered by justice, that have been placed where our blindness has broken the thread of your will.

'May your will be done in the world and then peace will certainly descend upon the earth, for the angels said to us: "Peace on earth among men with whom he is pleased!" (Luke 2:14.)

'And if you said there is only one who is good, the Father, then there is only one will that is good: your Father's will.'

To live life

The Christian is called to live life, to swim in the light, to plunge into crosses, but not to stagnate. At times our life is exhausted, our intelligence is clouded and our will undecided, because educated in this world, we have been used to living an individualistic life, which is in contradiction to the Christian life.

Christ is love and a Christian must be love. Love generates communion: communion as the basis of the Christian life and as its summit.

In this communion a person no longer goes to God alone, but travels in company. This is a fact of incomparable beauty that makes our soul repeat the words of the Scripture: 'Behold, how good and pleasant it is when brothers dwell in unity!' (Ps. 133:1.)

Fraternal communion is not, however, a static happiness, it is a perennial conquest with the continual result not only of the preservation of communion, but also of its expansion among many people, because the communion spoken of here is love, is charity, and charity spreads by its nature.

How often, between those who have decided to go united to God, unity begins to weaken, dust creeps in between one soul and another and the enchantment is broken, because the light that had emerged among them all slowly goes out! This dust is a thought, an attachment of the heart to oneself or to others; love of self for self and not for God, or of a neighbour or neighbours for themselves and not for God. At other times, it is withdrawal of the soul that had previously given itself to others, a concentration upon one's own self, one's own will and not on God, on our brother or sister for God, on the will of God.

And very often it is through a faulty judgment of someone who lives with us.

We had said we wanted to see only Jesus in our neighbour, to deal with Jesus in our neighbour, to love Jesus in our neighbour, but now we recall that a neighbour has this or that defect, has this or that imperfection.

Our eye becomes complicated and our being

is no longer illuminated. As a consequence, erring, we break unity.

Perhaps that particular neighbour, like all of us, has made mistakes, but how does God view him? What really is his condition, the truth of his state? If he is reconciled with God, then God no longer remembers anything, he has wiped out everything with his blood. So, why should we go on remembering?

Who is in error at that moment?

I who judge or my neighbour?

I am.

Therefore I must make myself see things from God's viewpoint, in the truth, and treat my neighbour accordingly, so that if, by some mishap, he had not yet sorted things out with the Lord, the warmth of my love, which is Christ in me, would bring him to repentance, in the same way that the sun dries and heals over many wounds.

Charity is preserved by truth, and truth is pure mercy with which we ought to be clothed from head to foot in order to be able to call ourselves Christians.

Does my neighbour come back?

I must see him new, as though nothing had happened, and I must begin life together with him in the unity of Christ, like the first time, because nothing remains. This trust will safeguard him from other falls, and I too, if I use this measure with him, may hope to be judged by God one day with the same measure.

Often love is not love

S ince in the world often love is not love, the saying is true: love is blind. But if a soul begins to love in the way God teaches (God who is love), it will very soon see that love is light.

Anyway, Jesus said it: 'He who loves me will be loved by my Father, and I will love him and manifest myself to him.' (John 14:21.)

A whirl of voices from the most varied sources often floods our soul, especially when it does not know what it means to love God. They are soundless voices but strong: voices of the heart, voices of the intellect, voices of remorse, voices of regret, voices of the passions . . . and we follow now one, now another, filling our day with acts that express, or are at least in some way determined by, these voices.

That is why sometimes, despite living in the grace of God, our life has only brief patches of sunshine, and the rest of it is immersed in a boredom which one voice, stronger than the others, often rises to condemn – as if to say this is not the true life, the full life.

If instead the soul turns to God and begins to love him, and its love is true, practical, active in every moment, then among the many voices that accompany life, it notices, from time to time, one voice.

More than a voice, it is a light that gently breaches the intricate concert of the soul. It is an almost imperceptible thought that offers itself to the soul, which is perhaps more delicate, more subtle, than the others.

This is, at times, the voice of God.

Then the soul that has decided to follow the Lord, that does not bargain with him but wants to give everything to him, draws off this clear and serene spring from the marshland: it is a sapphire among so many stones, it is gold among dust.

It takes it, it cleans it, it puts it in light, it translates it into life.

And if it happens that the soul has decided to go to God with other souls, so that the Father may rejoice in the brotherly love of his children, the soul (having taken advice from the person who represents God on earth for it) communicates with discretion its treasure to others. It does this so that the treasure may become a common possession, that the divine may circulate and, as in a competition, one soul may learn from another how to love the Lord better.

In this way the soul has loved twice: it has loved by putting God's will into practice, and it has loved by communicating with its brother and sisters. And God, faithful to his eternal words, will continue step by step to manifest himself.

All of this is highly desirable, so that all day long our heart may be immersed solely in thoughts of heaven, to the point of overflowing, and our life, nourished by the sacraments, will be deified.

You give God if you have him; and you have God if you love him.

Then in the world which is dark and dull there can be lit tiny suns which will point out the path to many. Suns which will give warmth, in the utter humility of their lives that are completely sacrificed to the Lord; where they do not speak, but he speaks; where they do not live, but he lives.

When unity is complete

When unity with our brothers and sisters is complete, when it has flowered anew and more fully from difficulties, then, as night fades into day and tears into light, often, I find you, Lord.

Going back into the temple of my soul, I meet you; or as soon as circumstances leave me alone, you invite me, you draw me, gently but firmly, into your divine presence.

Then you alone rule within me and outside me, and the house you have given me to use for the pilgrimage of life, feels to me, and I call it, the dwelling place of my God.

This presence of yours is love, but a love that the world does not know . . .

The soul is immersed as if in some delicious nectar and the heart seems to have become the chalice that contains it.

The soul is all a silent song known only to you: a melody that reaches you because it comes from you and is made of you.

These are the moments when peace seems something substantial, in which the certainty of salvation is absolute, in which, though still on earth, the soul seems to be swimming in heaven.

And . . . strangely – strange to the human way of thinking – we have gone out to our brothers and sisters all the day long, and in the evening, we have found the Lord, who has dissolved every trace, every memory of creatures.

It seems unnecessary in these moments to have faith, faith in his existence.

He, sweetly permeating our house, become our portion and our inheritance, he himself tells us of his existence.

Once we have known God

Once we have known God, when we fail to deserve his light because we have not been vigilant in love, and have let ourselves be overwhelmed by the cross without taking advantage of grace, the soul gropes in darkness and in anguish, and it seeks him.

The soul seeks Love, calls for it, cries out to it, screams at times and wails. But it does not find Love. It does not find Love because it does not love.

God does not yield. He has an immutable law. *Heaven and earth will pass away* . . . (Mark 13:31) and his words allow no exceptions.

The soul has no right to love before it loves: it receives love when it has love.

God has made it in his image and likeness, and he respects the dignity with which he has clothed it.

It is the soul that must take the initiative and love, almost as if making the first move in response to grace. Then God comes. He manifests himself to the one who loves him, gives to who has, and such a one will remain in abundance.

The soul that loves participates in God and feels itself to be lordly. It fears nothing. Everything gains value for it.

We pass from death to life when we love.

Still more beautiful

The War-horse

He paws the valley, and exults in his strength;
he goes out to meet the weapons.
He laughs at fear, and is not dismayed;
he does not turn back from the sword.
Upon him rattle the quiver,
the flashing spear and the javelin.
With fierceness and rage he swallows the ground;
he cannot stand still at the sound of the
trumpet.
When the trumpet sounds, he says, 'Aha!'
He smells the battle from afar,
the thunder of the captains, and the shouting.
(Job 39:21-25.)

If we open the Scriptures and read in the Old Testament how God describes some of the animals, we realize that no poet or painter has ever sung of them or painted them in such a vivid or wonderful way.

The eye of the One who created them was needed to inspire such majestic descriptions. Perhaps our own eye is not trained to see beauty, or it only sees beauty in a certain sector of human, and natural, life. For *we have not trained the soul.*

When a young country girl goes to town, even though she is always in touch with nature which is rich with traces of God, she dresses in the strangest of colours, with a disharmony that offends the eye. For her this is beauty, and the greatest works of art have little value, or none at all, *because she does not understand them.*

But in God's sight, where is the greatest beauty: in the child who looks at you with innocent little eyes, so like the clarity of nature and so lively; or in the young girl who glistens with the freshness of a newly-opened flower; or in the wizened and white-haired old man, bent double, almost unable to do anything, perhaps only waiting for death?

The grain of wheat so promising when, slenderer

than a wisp of grass, and bunched together with fellow grains that surround and form the ear, it awaits the time when it will ripen and be free, alone and independent, in the hand of the farmer or in the womb of the earth: it is beautiful and full of hope!

It is, however, also beautiful when, ripe at last, it is chosen from among the others because it is better than they, and then, having been buried, it gives life to other ears of wheat – this grain that now contains life itself. It is beautiful; it is the one chosen for future generations of harvests.

But when, shrivelling underground, it reduces its being almost to nothing, grows concentrated, and slowly dies, decaying, to give life to a tiny plant that is distinct from it and yet contains the life of the grain, then, perhaps, it is still more beautiful.

All various beauties.

Yet one more beautiful than the other.

And the last is the most beautiful of all.

Does God see things thus?

Those wrinkles that furrow the little old woman's forehead, that stooped and shaky gait, those brief words full of experience and wisdom, that gentle look of a child and a woman together, but better than both, *is a beauty we do not know*.

It is the grain of wheat which, being extinguished, is about to burst into a new life, different from before, in new heavens.

I think God sees thus and that the approach to heaven is far more attractive than the various stages of the long journey of life, which basically serve only to open that door.

As a heavenly plane sloping

Mary is not easily understood even though she is greatly loved. In a heart that is far from God, one is more likely to find devotion to her rather than to Jesus.

She is universally loved.

And the reason is this: it is Mary's nature to be *Mother*.

Mothers, in general, are not 'understood', especially by younger children; they are 'loved'. And not infrequently, indeed often, one hears that an eighty year-old man dies saying as his last word: 'mother'.

A mother is more the object of the heart's intuition than of the mind's speculation. She is more poetry than philosphy, because she is too real and profound, close to the human heart.

So it is with Mary, the Mother of mothers, who the sum of all the affection, goodness, and mercy of all the mothers in the world cannot manage to equal.

Jesus, in a certain sense, *confronts* us more: his divine and splendid words are too different from ours to be confused with them. Indeed they are a sign of contradiction.

Mary is peaceful like nature, pure, serene, clear, temperate, beautiful – that nature which is distant from the world, in the mountains, in the open countryside, by the sea, in the blue sky or the starry heavens. She is strong, vigorous, harmonious, consistent, unyielding, rich in hope, for in nature it is life that springs up perennially generous, adorned with the fragrant beauty of flowers, kind in the abundance of its fruits.

Mary is too simple and too close to us to be 'contemplated'.

She is 'sung' by hearts that are pure and in love, who express like this what is best in them. She brings the divine to earth as gently as a heavenly plane sloping from the dizzy heights of heaven to the infinite smallness of creatures. She is the Mother of all and of each human being, who alone knows how to burble and smile at her child in such a way that, even though it is small, each knows how to enjoy her caress and respond with its love to *that* love.

Mary is not understood because she is too close to us. She, who was destined from Eternity to bring graces, the divine jewels of her Son, to humanity, is there, near to us, and waits, always hoping for us to notice her gaze and accept her gifts.

If anyone is fortunate enough to understand her, she carries them off to her kingdom of peace, where Jesus is King and the Holy Spirit is the life-breath of that heaven.

There, purified of our dross and illuminated in our darkness, we will contemplate her and enjoy her, an added paradise, a paradise apart.

Here, let us be found worthy of being called along 'her way' to avoid staying always immature in spirit, with a love that does not go beyond supplication, petition, request and self-interest, but knowing her a little, may we glorify her.

One city is not enough

I f you want to win over a city to the love of
Christ,
if you wish to transform a town,
into the kingdom of God,
first make your plans.
Gather round you friends who share your
feelings,
unite yourself with them in the name of Christ
and ask them to put God before anything else.
Then make a pact with them:
promise one another constant and perpetual
love,
so that the Conqueror of the world
may be always among you
and be your leader;
so that when your ego has been destroyed in
love,
your every step may be sustained, your every
tear be dried,
by the Mother of the Beautiful Love.

Then size up the city.
Seek out its spiritual head.
Go with your friends to see him.
Present your plans to him, and if he does not
      consent,
do not take even a step, for otherwise you will
      ruin everything.
If he advises you and offers you some guidelines
accept them as a command
and make them an order for you and for your
      friends.
Assure him of your loyalty
for Christ has commanded it,
and offer to help him
– with your spiritual contribution –
in his heavy responsibility.
Then look for the poorest, the destitute,
the forsaken, the orphans, the prisoners.
Without pause in your action
run with your friends to visit Christ in them, to
      comfort them,
to reveal to them that the love of God is close
      to them
and watches over them.
If someone is hungry take food to him,

If you have no clothing or food,
ask for them from the Eternal Father with
faith,
because they are necessary for his Son Christ,
who you wish to serve in every human being.
And he will hear you.
Loaded with all these goods go through the
streets,
go up into attics and down into cellars,
seek out Christ in public and private places,
at the stations, along the railways, in the slums,
and caress him above all with your smile.
Then promise him eternal love,
so that the places you are unable to go,
may be reached by your prayers and your
sufferings,
united to the Sacrifice of the altar.
Leave no one alone,
and do not be sparing in your promises,
because you go in the name of the Almighty.
While you are gladdening the Lord in your
brothers and sisters,
God will concern himself with filling you and
your friends
with heavenly gifts.

Share these with one another,
so that the light may not grow dim and love go
    out.
If your action is determined
and your speech filled with wisdom,
many will follow you.
Divide these people into groups
so that with them you may leaven the city
that you wish to undermine with your love.
Keep going.
If others, having got to know your life
and seen with their own eyes the gifts you
    have,
ask you to talk, then speak,
but let the core of your speech be the things
you have learned from life.
Base what you say
on the teaching of the Church and on Scripture
which you and your group have absorbed,
as your first, safe, inexhaustible, eternal source.
So that, if the Shepherd speaks
you may be his living word.
Having consoled, helped, enlightened, made
    happy,
those who were the dregs of society,

you have laid the foundations
of the building of the new city.
Then gather your friends together and repeat
the beatitudes to them,
so that they may never lose the spirit of Christ
and of his preferences.
After that look further afield and tell everyone
that every neighbour,
rich or poor, beautiful or ugly, gifted or not,
is Christ who passes by.
Let your *task force*, the *task force* of Jesus, of
Mary,
be at his service, and each of you weep with
those who weep,
rejoice with those who rejoice,
constantly share sufferings and joys
with any sacrifice, without ever ceasing.
Alternate your action
with the deepest prayer,
lifted up by your army in perfect unity,
so that – through Christ –
there may be won the greatest glory from that
place.
And if the struggle costs,
know that there lies the secret of success,

and that he who urges you on has paid with his
    blood.
Forgive and pray for those who think ill of you,
for if you do not forgive, you will not find
    mercy.
And if suffering consumes you, sing out:
'*Behold my spouse, my friend, my brother*',
so that in the hour of your death
the Lord may say to your soul:
'*Arise, and hurry, my friend, my dove,
my fair one, and come away.*' (cf. S. of S. 2:10.)

Do this for a city until victory,
to the point, that is, that good overcomes evil
and Christ through us can repeat:
'I have overcome the world.' (John 16:33.)

But with a God who visits you every morning,
    if you wish,
one city is too little.
He is the one who has made the stars,
who guides the destiny of the ages.
Come to an agreement with him, and aim
    further:

at your country, at everyone's country, at the
   world.
Let your every breath be for this;
for this your every action;
for this your resting and your moving.

Having reached the other side, you will see that
   which has most value,
and you will find a reward proportionate to
   your love.
Act in such a way that in that hour you will not
   have to be sorry
for having loved too little.

Virgins today

A longside its many discoveries, innova-
tions and newly-created needs, technical
and otherwise, the world today also offers new
forms of the life of the spirit, which were not
thought of until quite recently, but now take
their place beside those that have developed
over the centuries and are always relevant.

Through the Secular Institutes, for example,
the life of perfection, of consecration to God, is
spread out in the midst of the world rather than
enclosed in monasteries and convents, that
have been, and still are, God's fortresses.

This is progress. It is a fact that points to a
greater maturity, and if on the one hand, this
shows the love of God for humanity, which
continues to thirst for what is pure and divine
and which the virgin is called to serve, on the
other hand, this shows, despite the terrible
aberrations of our century, the great trust God
has in his creatures, a trust which is supported
of course by adequate graces.

Today a virgin consecrated to God may find herself in jeopardy in the midst of the world, in offices, in schools, on buses, in cafes. For despite the fragility of her sex, she no longer wears a veil to protect herself or has the walls of a convent that can guard her, nor the grille, nor the time-table of the community that regulates life and is a restraint and a help, nor the ever vigilant eye of a superior.

Fewer external safeguards, therefore, can help her dedication and her promise, and therefore inner strength is needed, which in the midst of the world will detach the virgin from the world and keep her constantly united to the One whom she had chosen, or rather the One who has chosen her as his bride and who is by nature incompatible with the world.

She no longer has the attraction of the cloister, the silence, the enclosure to enhance the consciousness of her dedication. But there remains for her, as a comfort and an encouragement and an example, an incomparable fact, a star for her journey, that surpasses by far every other light: the Virgin of virgins – she who excels in beauty and dignity, in sanctity and grace, not only all human beings but all the angels, and whom both acclaim Queen.

Mary lived among people in the midst of the world and yet there never was, nor ever will be a creature more united to the Lord.

In our days it is she who shows virgins the secret of how to be perfect, of how to ascend to God, even amidst the bewilderment of the world.

There is a way which is Mary's: she is both Virgin and Mother. She is the Mother of her Son, and through him the Mother of the human race. For the virgin who follows Mary's way, her convent takes on the dimension of the world. Like a fountain of clear water, she is full of maternity towards souls, because she is pure, shining, the living image of God, who is Love. She is almost an incarnation of love, the arms of Providence outstretched to serve humanity, to dry tears, to heal wounds and to point out the Eternal.

There was nothing special about the clothes the Virgin Mary wore. She wore the clothes of her time, so that today's virgin, looking at her, does not feel she is falling short in any way when she dresses like everyone else. In fact these clothes, which she tries to keep as close as possible to the fashion of her time, a fashion she no longer follows for her own sake but for the sake of others, become dear to her: they let her heart inflamed with the love of God draw near to those who do not know him. They become a means to fulfil her mission, an instrument with which to fight for the Lord, and since the end is excellent, the means also is loved.

The Virgin Mary did not have other virgins as companions to live with. She was alone with God: with God before the incarnation, with God the Son after the nativity and with God in heaven after the ascension.

Because of this solitude she never lost contemplation; on the contrary, solitude actually favours mystical union with the Lord.

Virgins today, whom God has scattered through this dark world, like small stars in a night sky, are alone.

They are alone not because they are not loved by others, for in fact the words of the

Scriptures may often be truly applied to them: 'For the children of the desolate one will be more than the children of her that is married' (Isa. 54:1), but only because, as Jesus himself said of virginity: 'Not everyone understands'. (cf. Matt. 19:11.) It is precisely in what is most sacred and most beautiful in them that virgins are not understood and, indeed, because of the hatred of the world, at times are despised. And in this they find a source of tears and suffering, which can make their spiritual motherhood fruitful and guarantees that they are working for the Eternal, for the One who, himself a Virgin, died on the cross and drew all to himself. The virgin in the world is beautiful in her solitude. Because she is alone, she is united to God, and because she is united to God, she is raised high and set apart. Raised high and set apart for a greater embrace of humanity; and she benefits many as did her Spouse who has impressed on her heart the stamp of supernatural love.

And, with her existence alone, she witnesses to a balance that Christianity has restored: the equality of men and women. For if a man who has chosen celibacy is something special, the beauty is double in the case of a woman, inasmuch as she would be naturally inclined to lean upon man. As a newly open flower cut and offered at the altar, she sings the greatness of the human soul which is made for heaven, that heaven in which we will not be so much like men and women, but like angels.

And to have an idea of how beautiful a virgin is, it is enough to think how God considers her.

If in the Church in the course of the centuries the Lord wished to reveal a secret for the whole of the human race, to dictate a message, to manifest a desire he had, often he turned to virgins as the most trustworthy confidants. They have been almost antennae that receive the divine. Sacrifice and love have made them particularly sensitive and like 'another Mary', they have distributed, as handmaids of the Lord, through the Church, the gift to their brothers and sisters.